COLONIAL PEOPLE

The Tailor

Wauconda Area Library
801 N. Main Street
Wauconda, IL 60084

CHRISTINE PETERSEN

mc **Marshall Cavendish**
Benchmark
New York

Website: www.marshallcavendish.us

This publication represents the opinions and views of the author based on Christine Petersen's personal experience, knowledge,
and research. The information in this book serves as a general guide only. The author and publisher have used their best efforts
in preparing this book and disclaim liability rising directly and indirectly from the use and application of this book.

Other Marshall Cavendish Offices:

Marshall Cavendish International (Asia) Private Limited, 1 New Industrial Road, Singapore 536196 • Marshall Cavendish
International (Thailand) Co Ltd., 253 Asoke, 12th Flr, Sukhumvit 21 Road, Klongtoey Nua, Wattana, Bangkok 10110,
Thailand • Marshall Cavendish (Malaysia) Sdn Bhd, Times Subang, Lot 46, Subang Hi-Tech Industrial Park, Batu Tiga,
40000 Shah Alam, Selangor Darul Ehsan, Malaysia

Marshall Cavendish is a trademark of Times Publishing Limited

All websites were available and accurate when this book was sent to press.

Library of Congress Cataloging-in-Publication Data

Petersen, Christine.
The tailor / Christine Petersen.
p. cm. — (Colonial people)
Includes index.
Summary: "Explore the life of a colonial tailor and his importance to the
community, as well as everyday life, responsibilities, and social practices
during that time"—Provided by publisher.
ISBN 978-1-60870-417-0 (print)
ISBN 978-1-60870-639-6 (ebook)
1. Tailors—United States—History—17th century—Juvenile literature.
2. United States—History—Colonial period, ca. 1600-1775—Juvenile literature.
I. Title.
GT5960.T28P48 2012
646.400973'09032—dc22
2010016864

Editor: Joy Bean
Publisher: Michelle Bisson
Art Director: Anahid Hamparian
Series Designer: Kay Petronio

Expert Reader: Paul Douglas Newman, Ph.D., Department of History, University of Pittsburgh at Johnstown

Photo research by Marybeth Kavanagh

Cover photo by National Geographic/Getty Images

The photographs in this book are used by permission and through the courtesy of: *North Wind Picture Archives*: 8, 10, 12, 19;
Nancy Carter, 4. *Christopher Coleman*: 16. *Michelle Thompson*: 21. *The Image Works*: Jeff Greenberg, 23; Mary Evans Picture
Library, 27; SSPL, 34. *The Colonial Williamsburg Foundation*: 28, 32, 38. *Corbis*: Geoffrey Clements, 35. *Alamy*: North Wind
Picture Archives, 41; World History Archive, 43.

Printed in Malaysia (T)
1 3 5 6 4 2

CONTENTS

ONE   Coming to America 5

TWO   Learning the Trade 14

THREE   The Perfect Fit 20

FOUR   The Colonial Tailor's World 30

FIVE   Changing Times 37

Glossary 44

Find Out More 45

Index 46

ONE

Coming to America

Many tales of English colonization in North America focus on early settlers' desire for fortune, land, and personal or religious freedom. These ideals were the seeds that grew into a diverse and independent nation. Yet none of these reasons explain why English settlers first decided to try to establish an American colony. It began with a simple plan—to sell more wool.

Wool is a type of sheep's hair. The English bred many varieties of sheep, and each type had a slightly different color or texture of wool. Over centuries the English wool industry became complex. Different groups of **craftsmen** specialized in each step of the production process. The weaver made woolen material on a giant loom, which crossed over strands of yarn to make different patterns. The most tightly woven woolens could resist water.

Like every task in colonial America, the production of yarn from raw wool was done by hand—usually by women and children.

Woolen materials were sometimes brushed after looming. These were perfect for making blankets or sweaters. The brushed wool was loose, with many air spaces between the fibers. Body heat passed through the material and became trapped in these spaces, keeping a person warm. When woven with other threads, such as silk, wool became very soft. Wetting, heating, and pounding made wool thicker. This was the job of the **fuller**. The dyer used dyes made from plants or minerals to add colors and patterns to the finished material. People could buy wool and other **textiles** in the shops of **mercers** and **milliners**.

Some people may have given little thought to the craftsmen who made the material they bought. But almost all people were familiar with their local tailor. The tailor took the finished material, made careful measurements, and sewed by hand the clothes people wore every day of their lives.

Competition

English merchants sold great amounts of wool at home, but since the twelfth century they also had shipped and traded wool and woolen materials around the world. In the sixteenth century, a competitor entered the scene: Spain. For a long time, Spain had been a poor nation that lived in powerful England's shadow.

Money from its up-and-coming wool trade funded the journey of Christopher Columbus in 1492. On that trip Columbus became one of the first known Europeans to explore the New World. He brought back gold, gems, and valuable plants that increased Spain's wealth and power. Spain established colonies in North America, and its trade empire soon stretched worldwide. English merchants could not sell as much wool as Spanish merchants, as the Spanish began raising sheep in their North American colonies. Spanish ships also controlled many sea routes. This made it hard—and dangerous—for English merchants to reach trade ports in Asia.

In 1584, explorers encouraged Queen Elizabeth I of England to authorize a colony on the Atlantic coastline of North America. Colonists would need to buy wool, which would help bring England's wool industry back to life. Meanwhile, an English colony also would keep Spain from becoming too powerful in North America. There were other arguments in favor of the plan. The deeply religious queen wanted to spread Christianity as widely as possible. She hoped to save the souls of American Indians and to increase the influence of the Church of England. In addition, American colonists might make use of the region's valuable natural resources, such as timber for building ships and iron for making weapons.

Merchant ships carried people and goods between England and the colonies.

With the queen's blessing, the explorers set off. Landing just south of the Chesapeake Bay on North America's central Atlantic Coast, they claimed a massive stretch of land and called it Virginia. But England's idea of a colony was more of a dream than a reality. The first settlers, all men, found it too hard to live in a foreign land. They left after just a year, before they could even establish farms.

Trying Again

Many English people still believed that Virginia could be colonized, but no lord or businessman was wealthy enough to fund the project alone. In 1606, some English merchants decided to share the cost of establishing a new colony. With a charter from the English Parliament, they formed a joint stock company that would provide ships, supplies, and settlers. The charter allowed the company to raise money by selling stock, or shares of the corporation. King James I gave the Virginia Company land in the lower Chesapeake Bay, and the planning soon began.

The first ships sailed through the Chesapeake in May 1607 and headed inland along a river. The settlers called it the James River after their king, and the colony became Jamestown. About half of these settlers were members of the **gentry**—English citizens with wealth and power. Gentlemen became the leaders of the colony, but

The settlers at Jamestown brought some supplies from England but had to build a new community when they arrived in Virginia.

they knew nothing about building houses, fixing tools, or healing injuries. For these tasks the company had sent along craftsmen, laborers, doctors, and a few young boys. William Love went along as Jamestown's first tailor.

None of the settlers were farmers, and wool was the last thing on their minds. Growing food was not much of a concern, either. They wanted to find gold. They also hoped to locate the Northwest

Passage, a water route believed to link the Atlantic and Pacific oceans. If someone found this passage, merchant ships could more quickly reach Asia to trade English goods for valuable spices and silk. Then, the settlers thought, everyone would get rich.

In January 1608, a second group of ships brought much-needed food supplies and a hundred more settlers—including six tailors—to Jamestown. As William Love had already learned, Jamestown tailors would do much more than make and repair clothing. They would serve as soldiers, farm and hunt food, and help with any other job that needed doing. This was the life of a colonist.

The Plant That Saved Virginia

More than half the early Jamestown colonists died from illness, starvation, or injuries from fights with local American Indians. They found neither gold nor any sign of a passage to Asia. England's colony might have failed yet again if not for a discovery made by the farmer John Rolfe. In 1612, Rolfe experimented with growing tobacco. This plant grew naturally in North and South America, and Columbus had introduced it to Europe. Tobacco smoking became popular in the late sixteenth century after a Spanish doctor said that tobacco had many health benefits. Rolfe knew that the leaves from the tobacco plant sold well in England,

Bought and Sold

Men who paid a fare to reach Virginia received a piece of land in return. The fares of his wife, children, and servants earned land as well. To get even more land, a man could pay for strangers to come and live with him and his family. There were plenty of ways to do this. Many poor people were willing to try life in America. In addition, the English government was eager to get rid of people who crowded the jails and poorhouses.

This was a winning situation for Virginians. A settler earned land, and the people he took with him became his indentured servants. Indenture was a contract. The landowner provided food, clothing, housing, and medical care. The servant worked off his fare over a period of years. Indentured servants were little more than slaves, however. Landowners could sell their servants to other colonists, and servants were punished severely for misbehavior. Indentured servants could pay off their contract in about seven years. Then they, too, would earn a piece of property from the government and a collection of tools with which to farm it.

Large landowners eventually found indenture inconvenient because they had to replace their workers every few years. Slaves, on the other hand, were a lifelong investment. Hardship was a reality of life for slaves. They rarely had enough to eat, and they slept in buildings that did not protect them from heat, cold, or bad weather. These conditions made slaves more likely to get sick and injured, and they were unlikely to get good medical care. Like indentured servants, slaves could be sold at any time. But slave families were far more likely to be separated when a sale occurred. Very few could ever hope to be free.

and he hoped tobacco farming would provide a source of income for the Jamestown colony.

Virginia's soil and climate were perfect for growing tobacco. Soon every independent Jamestown landowner was scrambling to plant his own crop of tobacco alongside foods such as corn and squash. More people came from England to take advantage of free Virginia land offered to tobacco farmers. Colonists traded barrels of tobacco, called hogsheads, for goods and services. And just as Rolfe had hoped, tobacco sold very well in England. Colonists used the money to pay for products they could not easily make in America. First among these products were textiles. Every colonist needed clothing—and he needed a tailor to make it.

TWO

Learning the Trade

With the arrival of six tailors in January 1608, there were suddenly more tailors in Jamestown than any other kind of craftsman. The situation was the same in England, where the wool trade was going strong and a large population created a demand for clothing. As a result, tailors represented the largest group of skilled workers in England. Simply because there was so many of them, it was likely that tailors would be found among any group of new settlers that arrived in America.

Young tailors had another good reason for moving to the colonies. In England, tailors were required to join a **guild**. These organizations controlled every aspect of the trade in their region, from sales to daily wages. Most young tailors had one ultimate goal: to become a master. A master was a highly experienced tailor with his own shop. He had status, a reliable income, and influence in the community. But most guilds already had several masters. They feared competition and allowed very few **journeymen** to join their ranks. When many young tailors thought of the possibility of life as a low-ranking employee, they decided the colonies would be a good place to start their own shops free from guild control.

One Stitch at a Time

England and the colonies had a similar system for training tailors and other craftsmen. A boy's education usually began by the age of eleven. He rarely chose his profession. In most cases he joined his father's trade, or his father chose something for his son that was available in their community. Training in a craft was called **apprenticeship**. The boy signed an indenture stating that he would behave and work hard. His new master also signed the contract. The master agreed to provide the boy's food and housing, and to teach him the secret skills of the trade. This relationship lasted as long as seven years. Some masters were kind, but many others were stern and unforgiving. No matter how well they got along, the master expected his apprentice to work throughout the day, just as he did. Sunday was their only day of rest.

A tailor's apprentice began his training by doing the simplest tasks around the shop. He started a fire in the hearth early every morning, swept the floors, and ran errands. Once the boy proved

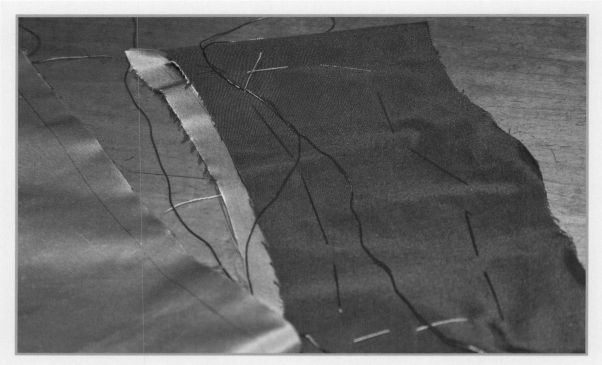

The apprentice tried out different types of needlework on leftover pieces of fabric before the tailor allowed him to sew a real garment.

himself reliable, the tailor had him collect a pile of **cabbage**. This was the tailor's term for small pieces of material left over after he cut a pattern. The master gave an ivory needle and thread to the apprentice, who practiced needlework on cabbage. The apprentice might start with a running stitch, which required simply passing the needle up and down through the material. This was a quick but strong stitch. It was perfect for sewing seams, which were necessary for almost every garment. Basting stitches were also important. These large stitches sometimes replaced pins when

A Woman's Place

Tailoring was always a man's trade, yet sewing was also considered a womanly art. Girls began learning needlework at a very young age. Poor and middle-class women used their sewing skills to make household linens such as napkins and dishcloths. Some also learned to sew simple garments, including shirts and aprons. Wealthy women never had to do such work, but they still spent a great deal of time with needle in hand. The ability to produce fine embroidery was considered the mark of a lady. Women decorated pillows and other items around the house, and they adorned clothing with gold thread and other colorful touches.

Few colonial women held paying jobs, though many worked in businesses owned by their husbands. For women who did need to make a living, sewing was a natural fit. Tailors sometimes hired unmarried women or widows as sempstresses. Young women could also be apprenticed to dressmakers. Milliners offered apprenticeships in which they taught girls how to run a women's clothing shop.

Colonial women directly helped a tailor's work by making the thread and cloth he used every day. Countrywomen spun the wool, hemp, and flax linen raised on their farms into thread, which they sold either to the tailor or to families that owned looms. Loom owners wove thread into cloth, which the tailor bought back and made into clothing.

holding pieces of material together temporarily. Tailor's tacking required similarly large, loose stitches. Tailors used these stitches to mark the lines of a pattern onto material. Unlike chalk marks, tailor's tacking never left stains and could be seen on both sides of the material. The apprentice did not tackle difficult buttonhole stitches until his skills were nearly expert.

Getting Ahead

Whatever his trade, an apprentice also studied reading and mathematics. Education was valued throughout colonial society, and these skills were important for a craftsman to run a successful business. The tailor's job required a few special skills. Unlike some other craftsmen, a tailor worked closely with his clients. He might even live in their homes for a while when completing a job. With this in mind, some masters taught apprentices to speak French. Many wealthy colonists considered French people very stylish, and they were impressed when a tailor could speak the language fluently. Etiquette was equally important. While colonial physicians rarely touched patients, the tailor measured his clients from head to toe. The best tailors knew how to make their clients relax at these times.

If a tailor's apprentice successfully learned the basic skills of his trade, his master promoted him to journeyman. Many journeymen continued to work alongside a master for a few years as they fine-tuned their skills. But they had freedom and a small income, and they might get married. Other journeymen did as their job title suggests—they traveled through the countryside to offer their services. In these years a journeyman could gain experience and save money. Eventually he might be ready to start his own shop and be called a master.

In colonial America, young boys went to school but their education continued even after they became apprentices.

THREE

The Perfect Fit

Colonists had only a few options when they needed new apparel. In cities, women could visit the milliner's shop to find ready-made items such as **shifts**, cloaks, and aprons. Men could order ready-made shirts and cloaks from England, but the shipping might take months. Rural colonists often chose to make simple garments by hand at home. Some grew flax or raised sheep to produce homemade linen and wool. This was less expensive than buying material, but it took a great deal of time and effort.

Colonial import records for the year 1721 show that 60 percent of the money colonists spent was for textiles. This was typical. Colonists who could afford material bought it and took it to the tailor. His expert work not only saved them time, but also made them look good.

What Should I Wear?

Male colonists moving to Virginia were advised to bring three shirts, one waistcoat (a long vest), several pairs of stockings and shoes, and a woolen hat. Shirts served double duty as nightgowns. If they could afford it, men were asked to bring three suits. A suit included knee-length **breeches** and a long coat. Typically, each suit was made of a different material. This gave men a choice of

These men wear a variety of colors and styles but also show the strict colonial dress code—jackets and hats are worn unless working.

garments depending on the day's weather or event. Suits made of sturdy material were worn when laboring—sometimes with a vest or apron in place of the jacket. Finer clothing was saved for attending formal events such as church services. This list was short and basic, but it met the needs of most colonial men.

Clothing was more varied for women, and styles changed over time. A woman's long linen shift served as both a nightgown and a slip. Made from the flax plant, linen was a sturdy material favored for undergarments and shirts because it could be boiled to remove stains and body odors without shrinking. Women laced a **bodice** over their chest. Seventeenth-century women usually wore petticoat skirts and a waistcoat with tie-on sleeves. In later decades colonial women sometimes chose one-piece dresses to wear at home.

Young colonial boys and girls wore simple dresses with aprons. Long bands of material called hanging sleeves were often attached to the shoulders of these dresses. These were designed as handles to hold children upright while they learned to walk. By the age of six, children found this style embarrassing. They wanted to wear clothing similar to that of their parents.

When getting dressed, colonists of all ages had to think about weather. They wore apparel made of heavy wool and linen in winter and chose light silks or blended materials for summer. Sleeved coats or hooded capes kept them warm and dry when they worked, walked, or traveled outside in bad weather. Colonists were also careful to protect their clothing from damage. Before riding horseback, men sometimes buttoned **sherryvallies** over their pants. Made of stiff material or leather, these garments caught mud that a horse's hooves kicked back onto the rider's legs. All but the wealthiest women wore aprons to protect their skirts from stains caused by cooking and looking after messy children.

Cold days call for extra layers of clothing, such as the coats and hooded cloaks worn by these colonists.

Make an Apron

When was the last time you wore an apron? You might have slipped one on when helping in the kitchen or doing an art project. But chances are, an apron is not among your everyday items of clothing. Colonial Americans were quite different. Women, children, and craftsmen wore aprons to protect their valuable clothing from stains and tears.

A woman's apron reached her knees and tied around her waist or ribs. Children's aprons were bibbed. They had an additional section of cloth over the chest, with ties at both the waist and the neck. Craftsmen could wear either type of apron. They might choose aprons made of coarse material or leather for durability and protection.

You Will Need

- A clean linen dish towel (16 by 24 inches (41 by 61 centimeters) is a common size)
- Your choice of needle and thread, or fabric glue
- Two yards of ribbon (3/4-inch (1.9 cm) wide) or sturdy cord
- A ruler
- A ballpoint pen
- Scissors
- A safety pin

Instructions

1. Hold the dish towel by its shortest side. Lay it on a flat surface with the seams facing up.

2. Align the ruler with the left edge of the dish towel. Measure 1.5 inches (3.8 cm) down from the top. (Remember that the top should

be a short side of the towel.) Use the pen to make a small mark at this point. Repeat on the right side of the towel.

3. Fold over the top of the towel at the marks to form a 1.5-inch band. This will be the casing to hold your ribbon or cord.

4. Sew the two layers of material using a needle and thread. Be sure to have adult supervision when using a needle. Make a line of running stitches along the seam of the towel, and tie off the thread at the end. You can also use fabric glue along the bottom edge of the casing. Keep the glue near the seam so it does not block the ribbon, and give the glue plenty of time to dry.

5. Choose ribbon or cord as a tie for your apron. Cut a length of 1.5 to 2 yards (1.4 to 1.8 meters), depending on your waist size; you can always shorten it later.

6. Insert the sharp point of a safety pin into one end of your ribbon or cord. Close the pin and insert it into an open end of the casing. Carefully thread it through the casing. It may help to hold the pin in one hand and gently bunch up the casing in the other as you work the safety pin toward the far end.

7. Remove the safety pin when it clears the far end of the casing. Pull the ribbon or cord through until it extends equally from each side.

8. Tie the apron around your waist. (Girls can raise it to their ribs.) Make sure the ribbon or cord is long enough to tie a large bow, and then trim any unneeded length. You can wash your apron by hand or in the washing machine, but remove the tie beforehand and reinsert it when the apron is clean.

Tools of the Trade

In England there were so many tailors that competition made them specialize their skills. Some did only a single step of the tailoring process. For example, the "table monkey" was a tailor at the lowest rank of the trade. He spent all of his time sewing. By contrast, the cutter was known among tailors for his ability to make patterns suited to each client. Other tailors concentrated on making apparel for particular customers—men or women, wealthy or middle class, and so on.

The colonial tailor worked under very different conditions. He often lived in a distant area and was the only person for miles around who could perform his craft. The tailor had to know every skill of his trade and provide every service for his clients. But there were no machines to speed up the work. He made each garment by hand, stitch by stitch and one tiny cut of the material at a time.

The tailor began by creating a profile of the client's body. He measured legs and arms, back and chest, waist and neck. He used a pattern to make the basic shape of a garment and then pinned or basted pieces of material over the body. Later he took these pieces to his table or workbench, located next to a window where sunlight helped him see as he worked. All of his tools were by his side, ready when needed. A metal thimble protected his thumb as he (or one of his apprentices or sempstresses) carefully sewed the garment with a threaded ivory needle. Seams and other tricky pieces were ironed to mold their shape on the garment. The iron had a metal trapdoor that held in a hot stone.

Some pieces of the garment required additional details before they could be attached. The tailor made tiny triangular notches

A colonist looks on as the tailor measures his wife for new apparel.

Sit Up Straight!

Colonial Americans had firm beliefs about posture. "As the twig is bent, so grows the tree," they said. Straight posture was considered a sign of good upbringing, and colonists started early to prevent their children from becoming "bent."

Many mothers wrapped their infants in tight swaddling bands soon after birth. Like little mummies, they were trapped with their arms held to their sides and their legs stuck out as straight as boards. The tailor fitted toddlers with stiff bodices. These garments contained stays, pieces of wood, leather, or hard baleen from the mouth of a whale. Parents laced the garments tightly around their toddlers' chests so their children would stand and sit rigidly upright. When they started wearing adult clothing around the age of five, boys stopped wearing stays. Waistcoats provided a tight fit to keep them standing tall. Most girls remained in stays for the rest of their lives. As adults they might even wear them to sleep and keep them on during pregnancy.

around the edges of collars and sleeves so they would curve without bunching. He used his sharp **bodkin** to punch buttonholes and to smooth their edges. He later strengthened the holes with tiny buttonhole stitches. The tailor might also thread ribbons through the eye of the bodkin and through the material as decoration. However beautiful his work, the tailor was not satisfied until a final test guaranteed that the garment was a perfect fit for its new owner.

The tailor would surely see these same clothes again in years to come. He might tighten the waist of a father's old breeches so the knee-length pants would fit a teenage son. He would insert diamond-shaped **gussets** under the arms of a shirt to make room for a broader chest. A simple triangular **gore** added to the front of a shirt made it looser around the waist. Colonists counted on every garment to last for a decade or more, despite the wear and tear it received. The tailor's fine work ensured that they were not disappointed.

FOUR

The Colonial Tailor's World

By 1732, England had established thirteen colonies along the Atlantic coastline of North America. Their total population, including African slaves, was greater than 630,000. By law, these colonies all belonged to England. In spirit, there were three groups of colonies, and each had their own culture. The lives of tailors in these three regions were so different that they might as well have lived in separate countries.

The southern colonies included Virginia, Maryland, North and South Carolina, and Georgia. Farming was the focus of this region, and the owners of large tobacco plantations held the greatest power. There were four middle colonies: New York, New Jersey, Pennsylvania, and Delaware. Many settlers there came from other European countries other than England. They spoke a variety of languages and represented several religions. Many were happy to live simple lives on their small pieces of land. But the middle colonies were also home to two of the largest colonial cities, New York and Philadelphia. These became major trade centers.

In New England the common bond was religion. The earliest settlers were Puritans in Massachusetts. The Puritans sought to establish a more strict religious community than they had found in England. The rules of this community were strict, and there was very little personal freedom. Later Puritans established the colonies of Connecticut, Rhode Island, and New Hampshire to allow common people a greater role in government. The city of Boston was the heart of this region. Its manufacturers produced many textiles, and merchants shipped them on Boston-made ships to ports in England and the Caribbean.

The Southern Colonies

Most southern colonists lived in the countryside. The tailor might keep a shop in a central village, where colonists could visit while doing other errands. But unless they could stay long enough for him to do fittings and to complete the work, it was often easier for the tailor to do the traveling. He packed up his tools, rode through the countryside, and stayed with each client along the way. Clients would order material and have it ready when the tailor arrived.

Tailors take advantage of light from the window as they work at the bench.

Most farmers needed clothing for only a few people. But the owners of large southern plantations had dozens of people under their care. When the tailor finished making apparel for the family, he began on garments for each slave. As English officials reported in 1721, "the slaves are cloathed with Cottons, Kerseys, flannel, and coarse linnens, all imported." The apparel of field-workers was often dyed blue—jackets and trousers for men, linen skirts with bodicelike jackets for women. These simple garments were easy and cheap to make, and they clearly marked the status of slaves should they choose to run away. Knowing that visitors would see his house slaves, the landowner often had the tailor refit clothes handed down from his family members. The most finely dressed slave was the owner's manservant. His colorful breeches, waistcoats, and jackets decorated with buttons and braids showed off his master's wealth.

The Middle Colonies

The middle colonies were home to two of colonial America's largest cities: New Amsterdam (later called New York) and Philadelphia. There were fewer slaves there than in the South, but the gap between rich and poor was noticeable to all. As colonists continued to move into the area, many found it hard to find jobs or land for farming. Wealthy colonists described these people as "mean," not because they were unkind but to show that they had low social status. "Meaners" were lucky to afford garments from secondhand shops. They had little time to worry about fashion anyway. The poor had to think about how to feed their families each day.

Meanwhile, the gentry were expected to look good at all times. Men dressed in waistcoats and jackets in any kind of weather. For

Workers soak material in red dye, a favorite color of colonial Americans.

business meetings and balls they had the tailor make garments of satin and velvet with detailed embroidery and lush lace at the collars and cuffs. Their wives read descriptions of the latest London fashions in English magazines and got reports from friends who traveled abroad. Women's formal **mantua** gowns were made with beautifully patterned material. The bodice was often open in front, and it laced tightly over the stays. The tailor made large wooden hoops that fit underneath the skirt and made the hips flare widely to the sides or back. The tailor needed to keep up with every changing whim of fashion. He went to London in person or ordered dolls done up in the latest styles. He showed these to clients and made patterns to copy them.

Bold and Bright

Colonists enjoyed colorful clothing, and a number of natural dyes were used to create colored and patterned textiles. Most dyes came from plants. People extracted yellow dye from marigold and goldenrod flowers. They crushed berries to make pinks and purples. The woody husks of walnuts, when ground, made a nice brown dye. Hunters favored this color as camouflage on their outdoor clothing. Red pigment came from crushed cochineal beetles, imported from Mexico. Puritans chose this color for their winter cloaks and capes.

Blue was also a popular color. This dye came from the indigo plant. For more than a century, indigo was imported to the colonies. Young Eliza Lucas of South Carolina changed that in the 1740s. She experimented with growing indigo on her father's plantations in South Carolina. After five years, Eliza produced strong plants and a beautiful indigo dye. This soon became one of the southern colonies' most profitable export crops.

New England

New England Puritans wanted their apparel to be simple and respectable. In 1634, a Boston court passed the first law against "fashions and costly apparel." In part the law was meant to keep Puritans humble, as fancy garments showed more concern for self than for God. But such laws also helped keep middle- and lower-class people in their place. For example, a 1651 Massachusetts Colony law denied colonists the right to wear expensive, decorated apparel unless their income was high enough. The tailor sometimes upheld these rules, but he knew his clients would buy their clothing from England if he would not fulfill their wishes.

FIVE

Changing Times

From the earliest days of Jamestown to the American Revolution, tailors were a large part of the colonial population. In 1703, ten of New York City's five thousand citizens listed their occupation as tailor. By the early 1770s, Philadelphia had 30,000 residents and 121 master tailors. Following the English tradition, some of these masters met to form the first colonial tailoring guild. The Taylor's Company of Philadelphia determined the pricing of tailors' work and set a wage scale for journeymen.

Getting By

A tailor's location partly determined his success. Cities were home to a lot of people, which meant a great number of customers for the tailor. But more people also meant more competition from others in his craft. Making well-made, attractive garments brought

This red velvet suit, with extensive gold embroidery, would be worn at a ball or other special event.

customers back to his shop repeatedly. Tailors used good manners and knowledge of current styles to attract clients from the gentry, who paid well for the tailor's talents and time.

To decrease competition, some city tailors found it useful to specialize. Like tailors in England, they began to make only certain kinds of clothing. By 1674, female dressmakers had taken over the production of women's mantua gowns. Tailors saw that more middle-class colonists wanted to look like the gentry, so some specialized in making dress apparel and left the production of everyday wear (often called "undress") to others.

Despite his skill and training, a master tailor rarely earned more than a carpenter or bricklayer. Journeymen tailors were sometimes so poor that they had to ask for public assistance. This could be embarrassing, because people who received money from the government were required to wear a large letter P on their garments. The sign told everyone that they were paupers.

Tailors who worked outside the cities sometimes owned land. Like many other colonists, they raised crops to feed their families. Farming could be an additional source of income when work was slow. In the South a farmer-tailor might raise tobacco, rice, or indigo. Northern farms were better suited to flax or sheep.

Changing Times

In 1754, a new type of clothing became important. England began a long war (the French and Indian War) with the French, who claimed land west of the colonies that spanned as far as the Mississippi River. Tailors were asked to make army uniforms for colonial soldiers who joined the fight. Soon after winning the war, England began to impose taxes on the colonists. This was done in order to collect money to pay back the debt left over from fighting the war. For example, the Stamp Act of 1765 imposed a tax on every item made of paper, including postage stamps, newspapers, magazines, and even legal documents. This law affected the tailor's personal income and business. Two years later the English government announced a new law called the Townshend Acts. These acts taxed many goods imported from England. Textiles were on the list.

Losing Control

England's Acts of Trade and Navigation, passed in 1660, put a tight fist around the colonial economy. Colonial merchants had to sell their products to England or its other colonies, no matter how much more another buyer might offer. The acts were detailed and strict. There was little room for merchants to argue:

> Under the penalty of the forfeiture of all such goods and commodities, and of the ship or vessel in which they were imported . . . no sugars, tobacco, cotton-wool, indigoes, fustic, or other dyeing wood . . . shall be shipped, carried, conveyed, or transported from any of the English plantations to any land, island, territory, dominion, port, or place whatsoever, other than to such other English plantations as do belong to his Majesty.

England wanted to restrict the colonies' trade with other nations. The government also wanted to limit colonists' production of goods so that they would have to buy from England. In the late seventeenth century English merchants began to feel threatened by America's growing textile industry. In response, the English government passed the Wool Act of 1699. This law prevented colonies from exporting the wool they produced. At the same time, colonists were always dependent on England for high-quality materials. This made them vulnerable to any taxes the English government chose to apply.

This was bad news for tailors because if colonists had to pay more for material, they would order fewer new garments. That meant less work for colonial tailors.

These new laws affected everyone, but colonists reacted to them in different ways. Some colonists were loyal to England, and they believed England was best suited to rule America. Others pointed out that the English constitution guaranteed citizens a voice in the parliament that made their laws. These colonists argued for a colonial representative to look out for their interests in Parliament. Tailors stood on all sides of this argument.

Other colonists felt it was time for a break from England. Their feelings went beyond anger or frustration with the English king and government. More and more, Americans valued a government that gave citizens a voice.

A colonist can choose from many different textiles at the mercer's shop.

Colonists showed their unhappiness with English control in several ways. For example, some people stopped buying imported goods and encouraged fellow colonists to buy products made at home. American women supported this practice by holding spinning bees. They met in each other's homes to spin thread, which was made into cloth that tailors could use instead of material purchased from England.

In July 1776, members of the Second Continental Congress signed the Declaration of Independence, which announced to England that the colonies intended to be free states. Many tailors left their shops to fight when the American Revolution began. Tailors not only fought, but also made and repaired uniforms for thousands of soldiers. The war dragged on for years. In 1781, English leaders finally surrendered. Two years later, King George III recognized his former colonies as an independent nation—the United States of America.

America's population grew quickly in the decades after the Revolution. For a while, tailors continued to make all of the clothing their communities needed. But the nineteenth century was a time of rapid technological change. In 1813, the first power loom was built in Boston. A large waterwheel ran the loom, which made textiles far faster than people could. Sewing machines, which became available in the 1850s, allowed housewives to make clothing at home more easily. Manufacturers also bought sewing machines and hired groups of sempstresses to make ready-made clothing that could be sold cheaply. Soon most Americans wore factory-made clothing. Only a lucky few continued to enjoy finely made clothing fitted by the hand of a tailor.

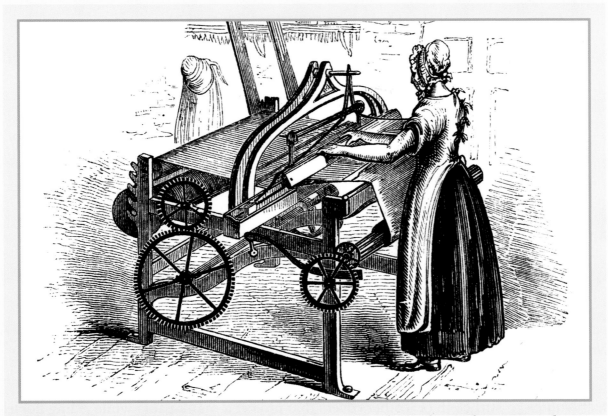

This woman is weaving cloth at a hand loom. In the eighteenth century these machines were gradually replaced by faster power looms.

Glossary

apprenticeship	the training of a person who works with an expert to learn a new skill or job
baleen	a hard substance that grows in the mouths of some whales
breeches	knee-length pants worn by colonial American boys and men
bodice	a tight-fitting women's undergarment or vest
bodkin	a needlelike tailor's tool used to make holes and to thread ribbons
cabbage	pieces of leftover material used by tailors' apprentices to learn sewing
craftsmen	trained workers who make objects by hand
fuller	a craftsman who processes wool to make it thicker
gentry	people who belong to a social class that has wealth and power
gore	a triangular piece of material used to increase the width of a garment
guild	an organized group of craftsmen
gussets	diamond-shaped pieces of fabric used to increase the size or strength of a garment
indenture	a contract requiring a worker to serve an employer for a certain number of years
journeyman	a craftsman who has completed apprenticeship
mantua	elaborate women's gowns
mercers	merchants who sell textiles
milliners	merchants who make and sell women's clothing
sempstresses	women who were paid to sew clothing in colonial America
shift	a shirt-shaped garment worn under women's clothing
sherryvallies	stiff cloth or leather covers that protect a man's pants while riding horseback
stays	pieces of wood or another unbending material inserted in a bodice to keep a person's posture straight
textiles	materials that are manufactured by weaving or other methods

Find Out More

BOOKS

Kalman, Bobbie. *A Visual Dictionary of a Colonial Community*. New York: Crabtree Publishing Company, 2008.

Lange, Karen E. *1607: A New Look at Jamestown*. Washington, DC: National Geographic Society, 2007.

Sills, Leslie. *From Rags to Riches: A History of Girls' Clothing in America*. New York: Holiday House, 2005.

Studelska, Jana Voelke. *Women of Colonial America* (We the People). Minneapolis: Compass Point Books, 2007.

WEBSITES

Colonial House

www.pbs.org/wnet/colonialhouse/history/index.html

This page, associated with PBS's television series *Colonial House*, offers interactive features, including a colonial dress-up game.

Colonial Williamsburg: Tailor

www.history.org/Almanack/life/trades/tradetai.cfm

Read a detailed account of the tailor's work and role in the colonial capital city of Williamsburg, and follow links to other interesting pages about colonial tailors and clothing.

Memorial Hall Museum

http://memorialhall.mass.edu/home.html

Click the "Dress Up!" link to see examples of clothing worn during different time periods in American history.

Index

Page numbers in **boldface** are illustrations.

American Revolution, 41–42

apprentice tailors, 15–16, 17, 18, **19,** 27

aprons, 23, 24–45

Boston, Massachusetts, 31

buttonholes, 18, 29

capes, hooded, 23, **23**

children, clothing of, 22, 24, 28

cloth, 5–6, **16,** 17, **43**

clothing, 20–25, **21, 23,** 28, **28,** 33–34, 43

coats, 23, **23**

colonies, English, 5, 7, 9–13, 30–36, 39-42

Columbus, Christopher, 7, 11

cutters, 26

dressmakers, 17, 38

dyers/dying, 6, **34,** 35

Elizabeth I (queen, England), 7, 9

farming, 10, 30, 33, 39

flax, 17, 20, 22

French and Indian War, 39

fullers, 6

gentry, 9–10, 33–34, 38

guilds, 14–15, 37

indentures, 12–13, 15

indigo, 35

Jamestown, Virginia, 9–13, **10**

journeymen tailors, 14, 15, 18–19, 37, 38

linen, 17, 20, 22–23

looms, 17, 42, **43**

Love, William, 10, 11

Lucas, Eliza, 35, **35**

mantua gowns, 34, 38

master tailors, 14, 15–16, 18, 19, 37, 38

men, clothing of, 20, **21,** 21–22, 23, **23,** 24, 28, 33–34 mercers, 6, **41**

middle colonies, 30–31, 33–34

milliners, 6, 17, 20

New England colonies, 31, 36

New York City, 31, 33, 37

Northwest Passage, 10–11

Philadelphia, Philadelphia, 31, 33, 37

poor people, 33, 38–39

posture, 28, **28**

Puritans, 31, 35, 36

Rolfe, John, 11, 13

sempstresses, 17, 27, 43

sewing machines, 42–43

sheep, 5, 7, 20

ships, **8**

silk, 6, 23

slaves, **12,** 13, 30, 32–33

southern colonies, 30, 31–33, 35

Spain, 6–7

spinners/spinning, **4,** 17, 42

stitches, 16, 18

suits, **21,** 21–22, **38**

table monkeys, 26

tailors
  in Jamestown, 10, 11, 13, 14
  training for, 15–19
  work of, 6, 26–29, **27, 28,** 31, **32,** 33–34, 37–39, 41, 42
taxes, 39–41

textiles, 6, 20, 39, 40, 41, **41,** 42

tobacco plantations, 11, 13, 30, 32

Virginia, 9–13

weavers/weaving, 5–6, 17, **41**

women, 17, 38, **43**
  clothing of, 20, 22, 23, **23,** 28, **28,** 34
wool, **4,** 5–7, 10, 14, 17, 20, 22–23, 40

yarn, **4,** 17

About the Author

Christine Petersen has written more than three dozen books and several magazine articles for a variety of audiences, from emerging readers to adults. Her subjects include science, nature, and social studies. When she's not writing, Petersen and her young son enjoy exploring the natural areas near their home in Minneapolis, Minnesota. Petersen is a member of the Society of Children's Book Writers and Illustrators.